**BFI FILM CLASSICS**

**Edward Buscombe**
SERIES EDITOR

**Colin MacCabe and David Meeker**
SERIES CONSULTANTS

Cinema is a fragile medium. Many of the great classic films of the past now exist, if at all, in damaged or incomplete prints. Concerned about the deterioration in the physical state of our film heritage, the National Film and Television Archive, a Division of the British Film Institute, has compiled a list of 360 key films in the history of the cinema. The long-term goal of the Archive is to build a collection of perfect show-prints of these films, which will then be screened regularly at the Museum of the Moving Image in London in a year-round repertory.

BFI Film Classics is a series of books commissioned to stand alongside these titles. Authors, including film critics and scholars, film-makers, novelists, historians and those distinguished in the arts, have been invited to write on a film of their choice, drawn from the Archive's list. Each volume presents the author's own insights into the chosen film, together with a brief production history and a detailed filmography, notes and bibliography. The numerous illustrations have been specially made from the Archive's own prints.

With new titles published each year, the BFI Film Classics series will rapidly grow into an authoritative and highly readable guide to the great films of world cinema.

Could scarcely be improved upon ... informative, intelligent, jargon-free companions.
*The Observer*

Cannily but elegantly packaged BFI Classics will make for a neat addition to the most discerning shelves
*New Statesman & Society*

Lobby card for the original release

**BFI** FILM

CLASSICS

# MEET ME IN ST. LOUIS

· · · · · · · · · · · · · · · · · · · ·

*Gerald Kaufman*

BRITISH FILM INSTITUTE

*bfi*

BFI PUBLISHING

First published in 1994 by the
BRITISH FILM INSTITUTE
21 Stephen Street, London WIP IPL

The British Film Institute exists
to encourage the development of film, television
and video in the United Kingdom,
and to promote knowledge, understanding and
enjoyment of the culture of the moving image.
Its activities include the National Film and Television
Archive; the National Film Theatre;
the Museum of the Moving Image;
the London Film Festival; the production and
distribution of film and video; funding and support for
regional activities; Library and Information Services;
Stills, Posters and Designs; Research,
Publishing and Education; and the monthly
*Sight and Sound* magazine.

British Library Cataloguing-in-Publication Data
A catalogue record for this book is available from the British Library

ISBN 0-85170-501-4

Designed by
Andrew Barron & Collis Clements Associates

Typesetting by
Fakenham Photosetting Limited, Fakenham, Norfolk

Printed in Great Britain by
The Trinity Press, Worcester

# CONTENTS

# ACKNOWLEDGMENTS

I am most grateful to Turner Entertainment Co for its generosity in giving me permission to consult its archive material on *Meet Me in St. Louis*. I am happy to record my gratitude, too, to Steve Hanson and Ned Comstock of the Cinema-Television Library and Archives of Performing Arts at the University of Southern California for the almost endless trouble to which they went in providing me with access to the *Meet Me in St. Louis* archives, and to Ned Comstock for seeking out further material for which I had not even asked.

G. K.

Judy Garland with Vincente Minnelli, adjusting the chandalier

## 'A MERRY LITTLE CHRISTMAS'
..........................

Remember this?

> Have yourself A Merry Little Christmas, it may be your last.
> Next year we may all be living in the past.
> Have yourself A Merry Little Christmas, make the Yuletide gay.
> Next year we may all be many miles away.
> No good times like the olden days, happy golden days of yore.
> Faithful friends who were dear to us will be near to us no more.
> But at least we all will be together if the fates allow.
> From now on we'll have to muddle through somehow.
> So have yourself a merry little Christmas now.

Surely that is not quite right? A good deal grimmer than memory – possibly faulty after all these years – recalls?

What we have here, as it happens, is the lyric that Ralph Blane in 1944 originally wrote for the Christmas song, 'Have Yourself a Merry Little Christmas', in *Meet Me in St. Louis*. Among others Judy Garland (and, after all, she was the one who was going to have to sing it), felt that as it stood the lyric was just too glum. So – although those original words would certainly have been much more suitable for use as ironic counterpoint during the execution scene of Carl Foreman's 1963 war drama *The Victors* – there was a speedy rewrite:

> Have yourself a Merry Little Christmas, Let your Heart Be
>   Light.
> Next year all our troubles will be out of sight.
> Have yourself a Merry Little Christmas, make the Yuletide gay.
> Next year all our troubles will be miles away.
> Once again, as in olden days, happy golden days of yore,
> Faithful friends who were dear to us will be near to us once
>   more.
> Some day soon we all will be together if the fates allow.
> Until then, we'll have to muddle through somehow.
> So have yourself a merry little Christmas now.

'Have Yourself a Merry Little Christmas' had to be brightened up because the intention, fully realised in the finished print which survives to delight us to this day, half a century later, was to make *Meet Me in St. Louis* the ultimate feel-good movie.

Feel-good? The miracle is that the picture ever got finished.

## ALI BABA'S CAVE

Drive along Jefferson Boulevard in Los Angeles; turn right on to Figueroa Street; turn right again into the private roadway of the University of Southern California; establish your identity with the security guard; park; walk along an avenue (in term-time, fighting your way through students milling around, selling craftwork from makeshift stalls, heading in droves for the

nearby cafeteria and bookshop, apparently doing anything but study); and you come to the impressive portals of the Doheny Library, named after an oil and real-estate magnate called Edward L. Doheny.

Climb the outer stairway; enter the building; establish your identity with another security guard; turn right; mount a staircase; walk along a corridor; and there you will find USC's Cinema-Television Library and Archives of Performing Arts, one of the great libraries of the world and an irresistible Ali Baba's cave for any devotee of film.

Here, among other precious documents, are the archives of the golden days of the MGM studios. In the Arthur Freed Collection and the Roger Edens Collection I found all the records of the preparations for, and filming of, *Meet Me in St. Louis*. Here were the original book by Sally Benson on which the film was based; several plot-treatments; several screenplays, all different and written by different authors; the film's budget and details of the salaries of all the participants; daily reports, in the most meticulous detail, of what happened every moment during filming; inter-office memoranda; letters relevant to the filming process; and a whole collection of miscellaneous documentation which throws fascinating light on what happened before, during and after the filming was completed. I spent days, deliriously happy, reading through this precious archive.

As I read, I was amazed at the vicissitudes through which Production 1317, as it was coldly listed in the studio files, had endured. Almost everything that could go wrong did go wrong, and things that could not conceivably have gone wrong went wrong too. Yet, thanks largely to the skill and affection lavished on the movie by a young (34) and relatively inexperienced director (*Meet Me in St. Louis* was only his third film and was his first full-length film in colour), Vincente Minnelli, we today treasure an immaculate work of art.

Starting in its issue of 14 June 1941, the *New Yorker* magazine published eight short stories under the title '5135 Kensington'. Their author, Sally Benson, added four more stories and assembled them in a book called *The Kensington Stories*. They dealt – each story covering a month of the year, from January to December – with events in Sally Benson's own life at 5135 Kensington Avenue, St. Louis, Missouri, in the years 1903 and 1904. For $25,000, Metro-Goldwyn-Mayer studios bought the rights to the book, not only for cinematic production but for radio and, perspicaciously, for television.

Lily Messenger – a Hollywood Scheherazade whose principal duty was to tell the stories of potential subjects for filming to Louis B. Mayer, head of production at MGM – supplied an initial treatment on 6 January 1942. Then work began on preparing a screenplay and, it seems, almost anyone who could put typewriter to paper was allowed to have a go. Two writers who were in particular demand were Howard Lindsay and Russell Crouse, Broadway playwrights who had written the smash hit based on family life, *Life with Father*; although regarded as the ideal authors of a screenplay about family life, they were in the middle of a new play and unavailable. If they had been free to become involved in the project, they would quite likely have written a competent screenplay; but it would not have been the *Meet Me in St. Louis* we have today.

Several teams and individuals did work on the film, sometimes at the same time, yet separately from each other. Sally Benson herself, in collaboration with Doris Gilbert, between 30 March and 9 May 1942 produced a treatment no fewer than 198 pages in length and, not wishing to spoil the ship for a ha'porth of tar, then supplemented this with additional material. Others who wrote screenplays between April and October 1942 were the husband-and-wife team Victor Heerman and Sarah Y. Mason (who had in 1933 jointly won an Oscar for their screenplay for another period family film, *Little Women*) and then William Ludwig (who had written several scripts about the Andy Hardy family as well as Margaret O'Brien's picture, *Journey for Margaret*, and who was later also to win an Oscar).

Then, however, there arrived on the lot the men who were eventually to come up with the screenplay that reached the screen. Irving Brecher, who had written films for the Marx Brothers, together with Fred Finklehoffe, who had worked on four musicals starring Judy Garland, on 30 April 1943 supplied a rough continuity outline, and then wrote a full screenplay; this was supplemented by additional work by Brecher alone, Finklehoffe having left for another assignment. Out of a pleasant collection of casual short stories Finklehoffe and Brecher eventually fashioned an immaculate screenplay, which was completed on 16 July 1943. The whole scriptwriting process cost MGM exactly $86,616.67.

Deciding that all the action should take place in one small corner of the city of St. Louis, Finklehoffe and Brecher established unity of place by eliminating previously planned scenes at Princeton University in New Jersey, and on a family visit to the Smith grandparents in Manitowoc, Wisconsin. They decided further that, with few exceptions, all the action should take place in the Smith home itself, and accordingly junked a scene at Mr Smith's office. They tidied up the plot structure, heightening the tension attached to the telephone call expected from Warren Sheffield in New York by turning Mr Smith's advance knowledge of the call into an ignorance which meant that, when the telephone rang, he took it off the receiver himself and rang off before Rose had the chance to speak.

They made Mr Smith's change of mind about moving to New York a private family affair by removing the maid Katie from those present when he announced that the family was to stay in St. Louis and eliminating her previously inserted comment of thankfulness, 'Bless the lord and all the saints.' They scrapped several romances in which Esther was to be involved, and eliminated a bigamous family called the Johnsons from the cast of characters. Instead of Mr Smith changing his mind as soon as objections to the move were made, they maintained tension and suspense by postponing his decision to stay until towards the end of the story, when the family had already packed and were about to leave. They almost totally eliminated a romance between Rose and a Colonel Andrews, with – in the completed film – the Colonel (renamed Daryl) trimmed down to only a few seconds of on-screen presence (when he rebuffs Rose's suggestion that they might meet again). They removed an almost inexplicable announcement by Tootie that she did not want to go to the fair. Along the way, too, instead of Rose having blonde hair and Esther black, they made the two sisters' hair auburn.

So at last the plot – spanning the cycle of four seasons – was settled upon. In St. Louis, Missouri, in the summer of 1903, the Smith family is awaiting impatiently the opening of the Exposition which, they are sure, will make their native city the centre of attention of the whole world. Mrs Smith is a contented housewife, happy to be under the thumb of her husband, Alonzo, a lawyer who is mostly out at the office. Meanwhile she engages in household tasks with Katie, the maid who is almost part of the family. Up in his bedroom Mrs Smith's father, who lives with his daughter, son-in-law and grandchildren, is happy to try on his collection of exotic hats in the intervals of dispensing wisdom and comfort to the rest of the household.

There is a son, Alonzo junior (Lon), who is soon to leave for Princeton University but meanwhile participates in the family's parties and music-making. Rose, the eldest sister, is generally flirtatious but anxious to wheedle a proposal out of her special boyfriend, Warren Sheffield, at present away in New York. Esther, in her late teens, has a crush on a new arrival next door, John Truett. Agnes and Tootie, both younger, play gruesome games involving lethal weapons and mortally sick – if not already dead – dolls.

Alonzo senior shatters the family's contentment by announcing that his lawyer's firm is to give him a promotion which will mean moving to New York. The family is aghast. Mrs Smith will lose her home, Katie will lose her job, Rose will lose her beaux, Esther will lose John Truett, Agnes and Tootie will lose their playmates. Still, reproved by their mother for ingratitude, the family accept their father's decision; but then Alonzo sees a distraught Tootie smashing her snowmen on Christmas Eve. He changes his mind; regardless of work prospects he will refuse the transfer. Rose and Esther will be left undisturbed to pursue their love-lives. The younger girls can go on playing their morbid games. As the story ends, in spring 1904, the whole family goes off to the Exposition grounds to celebrate the firework display which marks the inauguration of St. Louis' great moment.

The storyline was settled; but still there were problems about the characters' names. For reasons best known to herself, Sally Benson campaigned – unsuccessfully – for the character eventually called Lucille Ballard (Lon's girlfriend) to have the surname of either Picard or Dorsey. Esther's 'boy next door' began as Bluett, developed into Collins for legal reasons, and, despite objections from Sally Benson, ended up as Truett. Warren Sheppard, Rose's boyfriend, became Warren Sheffield. The daunting family whom Tootie was assigned to 'kill' on Hallowe'en, had – again for legal reasons – to have their name changed from Waughop to Braukoff. The maid was only permitted to be called Katie after the real-life Katie provided the New York office with a signed release. The final names were approved in a memo from Arthur Freed dated 11 December 1943.

Mr Alonzo Smith's name was not controversial but his character had to be protected from Sally Benson's depredations. An MGM inter-office communication dated 6 December 1943, signed by R. Monta and addressed to Arthur Freed, stated:

> We wish to transmit a suggestion made by Miss Sally Benson, to the effect that the father, Mr Smith, should be made a member of a wholesale dry goods firm or grocery firm which were then quite common in St. Louis, rather than a member of a law firm. She gives no particular reason except she believes too many pictures have been showing the father in the family as a lawyer, and we pass Miss Benson's suggestion on to you so that you may consider it.

Whether or not Miss Benson's suggestion was considered, Mr Smith remained a lawyer, even though there is hardly any reference in the film to his profession. Mr Smith's moral character was also protected from references in the book to his playing cribbage and drinking beer with cronies.

Yet while Benson's January to December structure was simplified to four seasonal episodes and several plot elements from the book were ditched – including Rose getting mixed up with a middle-aged man, Mother losing her temper, family quarrels – the tone of the book was retained and so were several key episodes. The opening of the picture, featuring all the family tasting the ketchup simmering on the stove, was expanded from one paragraph in the story to a whole sequence. A ride by Tootie with the man on the water-sprinkler became the ride on the ice-wagon. Tootie and Agnes creeping down the stairs at Lon's farewell party, together with Tootie singing 'I was drunk last night', come from the original stories. The tension that dominates the second half of the film, over Mr Smith's decision to move the family to New York, stems from just a three-page episode in the book. The last words in the book, as in the film, are 'I can't believe it. Right here where we live. Right here in St. Louis.' But in the book they are spoken by Agnes, while in the film they are given to Esther. The cakewalk is danced in the book, but again by Agnes, in a man's hat. The Hallowe'en sequence stems from a detailed section in one of the stories, though in the book it is Agnes (based on Benson herself) who takes the Waughop-Braukoffs. A passing reference to a trolley in the story for March gave birth to the trolley sequence and the Trolley Song.

Viewed from the hindsight of its international success and long-

Tasting the ketchup

lasting popularity, *Meet Me in St. Louis* has come to be regarded as having been adorned by a score which pioneered for the film musical, as *Oklahoma!* (in which MGM had invested, though the eventual film was not an MGM production) did for the Broadway musical, the concept that the songs should emerge from the action rather than be interpolated into the story as formal numbers performed on a stage. In fact, there had been many film musicals (*The Wizard of Oz* was just one) in which the songs both were part of the plot and advanced it.

Furthermore, *Meet Me in St. Louis* does not have a seamless score, as did the Garland vehicle *The Wizard of Oz* (songs by E. Y. Harburg and Harold Arlen) before it, and the Garland vehicle *The Pirate* (songs by Cole Porter) after it. Of the eleven main numbers planned for the film, six were arrangements of old songs which had been current during the period in which it was set. Another, 'Boys and Girls Like You and Me', had been written by Rodgers and Hammerstein for *Oklahoma!*; had been dropped from the Broadway production; was filmed for *Meet Me in St. Louis*; and was removed from the picture before release because it was felt to hold up the action.

Only four songs were composed specially for *Meet Me in St. Louis*, and one of these,'You and I', was supplied by the film's producer, Arthur Freed, with his long-time partner Nacio Herb Brown (who had together written, among many other numbers, 'Singin' in the Rain', which over the years popped up in numerous MGM musicals). Only three numbers were entrusted to the two men who got principal credit for the score, Hugh Martin and Ralph Blane, and their subordinate role in the production was scarcely surprising. They had up to that point written the songs for only one film, *Best Foot Forward*, a minor Arthur Freed musical (script by Brecher and Finklehoffe) with a military college setting; the most popular song from that score, 'Buckle Down Winsocki', is now almost forgotten. After *Meet Me in St. Louis*, Martin and Blane were to write songs for pictures that are today revived even less frequently than *Best Foot Forward*.

What is therefore remarkable is that the three songs they provided for *Meet Me in St. Louis* turned out to be three of the greatest numbers ever written for any movie. None of these songs – unlike 'You and I' – sought to mimic the style of the early Edwardian period in which the picture was set. The Trolley Song was a characteristic early 1940s number. 'The Boy Next Door' and 'Have Yourself a Merry Little

Christmas', though timeless in mood, were both much more ironic and knowing than genuine Edwardian songs about young love and about Christmas. What was special about these three compositions was that the Trolley Song provided exactly the right kind of exhilaration for Garland's one big production number in the film; that the other two fitted like gloves into the plot situations for which they were supplied; and that all three were perfect in every way: music married to lyrics as if their pairing was not just appropriate but inevitable. MGM, who never knowingly overpaid anyone, got a bargain for the $8,750 fee with which they recompensed Martin and Blane. For their part, Martin and Blane – like all other participants in *Meet Me in St. Louis* – found that they had stumbled into being collaborators in a classic.

Arthur Freed signed the final shooting script for *Meet Me in St. Louis* as 'complete' on 22 May 1943. It then had to be sent to the Hays Office censors, and on 30 July 1943 a letter from Joseph I. Breen of the Hays Office arrived at MGM:

Mr L B Mayer                                    July 29, 1943
Metro-Goldwyn-Mayer
Culver City
California

Dear Mr Mayer

We have read the temporary complete script dated July 21, 1943, for your proposed picture MEET ME IN ST. LOUIS, and are happy to report that the basic story seems to meet the requirements of the Production Code.

Page 13: The expression 'Mon dieu' is unacceptable.

Page 28: We presume that the expression '...there'd be h– to pay' will not be enunciated in full.

Page 77: In our judgment it will be unacceptable to show these youngsters throwing door mats and pieces of furniture they have stolen on Hallowe'en Eve, into a fire. Some other business should be substituted.

Page 107: The expression 'The Lord knows' is unacceptable.

Page 114: We presume that these bloomers, etc., will not include any intimate female garments.

Page 123: We presume this drinking will be handled with care.

Page 147: Since this is a family story, we must ask that the reference to a 'violation of the public morals code' be omitted, and some other charge be inserted. In this connection, we ask that the reference to the bedroom on page 148 be omitted. See also page 149, for the same. Some other charge should be found and the bedroom should not be mentioned as the locale.

We shall be glad to read changes which overcome these difficulties, and advise you further.

Cordially yours,

Joseph I Breen.

The censor was duly accommodated; although furniture was thrown on to the Hallowe'en bonfire, no indication was given that it had been stolen. Construction of the necessary sets was authorised. $151,575 was allocated for building the St. Louis Street. Designed by the Broadway designer Lemuel Ayers, it bore a remarkable resemblance to pictures of her childhood home in St. Louis that Sally Benson had sent to MGM. It was extremely expensive for its time; but the street earned its keep as a setting for many later MGM films – the house destroyed by Lucille Ball's mobile home in Minnelli's *The Long Long Trailer* was located there – and was also rented out to other studios. Another $62,225 was spent on the lower floor of the Smiths' house, $5,091 paid for the trolley tracks and $15,625 for the trolley depot. A miniature for the exterior of the World's Fair cost $16,625. A budget of $1,536,971.93 was set for the whole film, with a shooting schedule of fifty-eight days.

Casting was completed. Tom Drake, rather than Van Johnson for whom it had at first been intended, was given the role of John Truett. Robert Keith was considered as Mr Smith before Leon Ames was selected. Rehearsals began on 11 November 1943. Shooting started on 7 December. And then the troubles began.

There was a war on, and several minor members of the cast were lost as they were drafted into the armed forces. Joan Carroll (Agnes) and Margaret O'Brien (Tootie), being children, had to have a teacher on the set and this teacher, a formidable lady named Miss McDonald, was fiercely protective of them. On one occasion Miss McDonald demanded that Joan Carroll must leave the set, insisting that it was too late for her to go on working. On another day shooting had to be brought to a close because Miss McDonald insisted that Margaret O'Brien be sent home.

The services of Harry Davenport (Grandpa Prophater) had to be shared with the non-musical version of *Kismet*, which was being filmed on another set. Even when Davenport was present delays were caused, as on one occasion when his moustache and eyebrows were left in make-up. A considerable delay took place when the wardrobe department sent out two right shoes for Joan Carroll. Said a memo on another day: 'Wait for Margaret's hair to be dressed – wrong hair do because script clerk did not give right hair change to hairdresser.'

Accidents kept happening. A cameraman was hit on the head with a piece of carbon. A mishap to one of the performers on 31 March was the subject of a report by Dave Friedman, Assistant Director and, it seems, company spy. Friedman wrote:

> During the rest period for the extra talent on the St. Louis Fair set today, Miss Mary Broderick sat in a boardwalk carriage, which was on the stage for shooting purposes and not to be used otherwise. She leaned back too far, the carriage tipped over with her, and her head struck a light standard.
>
> Dr Jones examined Miss Broderick and found no injury, but Miss Broderick complained of feeling pain and requested a further examination. Dr Jones advised, as a final precaution, sending her to a doctor in Los Angeles for diagnosis and this was done.
>
> Time of injury: 10.25 a.m.
>
> Time of sending Miss Broderick to Los Angeles doctor: 11.45 a.m.
>
> Up to close of working day, 6.20 p.m., no further report on Miss Broderick had been received.

That was the last that was heard of Miss Broderick. Another Mary, Mary Jo Ellis, was among the daunting number of cast members who endured medical problems during the shooting, when she fainted on the set and had to be taken to hospital. Several actors and dancers fell ill. Harry Davenport, when present and not detained by *Kismet*, was also sometimes absent (forgivable, since he was 77) ill in bed; Tom Drake developed a 'hoarse throat'; Marjorie Main had a daily doctor's appointment; Leon Ames had to be treated for sinus and ear problems.

Four of the most important members of the cast were either struck down seriously or else caused major difficulties. On 2 February 1944, Joan Carroll (Agnes) was rushed to hospital for an emergency appendectomy. It was learned that she would be unable to work for two weeks, and her illness stopped shooting for several days. The caring studio making this warm-hearted film decided that she would not be paid salary during her 'period of incapacity'. However, Arthur Freed did send Joan flowers, for which this nice little girl responded with a fulsome thank-you letter. Mary Astor (Mrs Smith) developed a 'very acute sinus condition'. 'Recurring pneumonia' then followed, and in all she was away from filming for twenty-eight days.

It was, however, Margaret O'Brien (Tootie) and Judy Garland (Esther) who caused most of the delays, halting shooting for substantial periods and responsible for the production being prolonged by several days and going substantially over budget. Again and again there are references in Friedman's daily reports to the company 'not shooting' because O'Brien was not available. In addition to the absences enforced by Miss McDonald, O'Brien had tooth problems, which led to a crisis memo to Arthur Freed from one C. B. Allen:

> I understand that Mrs O'Brien has stated that because of the condition of Margaret O'Brien's teeth, it will be necessary that braces be prepared immediately, which could not be removed for a period of ten days, during which, of course, she would be unavailable for photography.
>
> I have talked to Dr Bronson, dentist, and it is his opinion, as well as the opinion of Dr Hickson, the dentist to whom he sent her for the purpose of preparing braces, that there is no immediate urgency, and that the braces may be prepared between pictures, or almost any time during the next several months. I understand that you have talked to Mrs O'Brien, and that she has indicated her willingness to have Margaret report for work

tomorrow, and I understand further that you will talk to her relative to deferring the contemplated dental work.

However, there was in fact an urgent need for dental work. The very next day, at 1.20 p.m., little Margaret's plate came loose and she had to be taken to the dentist. These problems, however, were small stuff compared with the full-scale panic which developed eleven days later, on 31 January. A memo to Fred Datig from Dave Friedman on 31 January panted:

> At 5.30 p.m. on Saturday 29 January, acting under Al Jennings' instructions, called the O'Brien home and gave Margaret O'Brien's call for Monday, 31 January. The conversation which was carried on with Miss Marissa O'Brien (Margaret's aunt) included description of scenes and scene numbers both for the St. Louis Street exterior set and the interior of the children's bedroom, cover set. At this time the call was accepted by Miss O'Brien for Monday's work and there was no mention made of Margaret being ill.
>
> At 4.30 p.m. on Sunday 30 January, Al Jennings called me at home to advise me that Marissa O'Brien had in turn called him at 4.05 p.m. to advise him that Margaret had been suffering with a combination illness of hay fever and influenza, and was also having nervous spells. He further told me that Marissa said at this time that the doctor in charge had advised that they take Margaret away for two weeks to recuperate from her illness, that Margaret would not be able to appear for work on Monday, 31 January, and that they were going to follow the physician's advice regarding the two weeks' rest.
>
> I got in touch with Mr Datig and asked him to check this information, and at 5.45 p.m. (Sunday) he advised me that he had called the O'Brien home and had been told by a woman who answered the phone that the O'Brien's [sic] had called her to tell her that they were at the railroad station and were leaving immediately for Arizona, and that they would advise her by wire to send necessary clothes, etc.
>
> I in turn transmitted this information to Mr Butcher and Mr Freed.

Due to the inclemency of the weather on Sunday and inasmuch as it had been raining, and Margaret O'Brien's departure had left us without a cover set, it was decided to cancel Monday's call for the exterior, which in turn left us without any work at all that we could do.

On Sunday night it rained again and more rain fell Monday morning, which in itself justified the cancellation of the exterior set.

Margaret O'Brien last worked with the Company on the morning of Friday, 21 January, between the hours of 9 a.m. and 11.30 a.m., at which time her work for the day was concluded and she was dismissed. On this morning she had a slight hoarseness, which Mrs O'Brien attributed to a hay-fever allergy to dirt.

Datig then sent his own memo to Freed, copied to almost everyone in sight:

Subject: MARGARET O'BRIEN

The above was given a cover set call for 10 a.m. today. At approximately 4 p.m. yesterday (Sunday) Marissa O'Brien, aunt of Margaret, called Al Jennings at his home and advised they were leaving today for Arizona as per doctor's orders due to the fact that Margaret had had a very bad cold and sinus condition, as well as other complications.

Al Jennings contacted Dave Friedman who, in turn, contacted me. At approximately 5.45 p.m. when I called their home I was told by the party who answered the phone that they had already left for Arizona. Also that Marissa had called the house from the depot some time before advising the party at the house that they would wire in today telling them where to send some clothes for Margaret. Up to 3 p.m. today no wire had been received and, since I am unable to find out who Margaret's doctor is, I can give you no further information at this time but will keep you posted.

Mr Sidney will advise whether or not she is to be paid salary during period of absence.

O'Brien had vanished. No one knew where she was. There then arrived, in a printed envelope from the California Limited train, posted in Kansas, a letter addressed to 'Mr Arthur Freed, Executive Bldg, c/o Metro Goldwyn Mayer Studios, Culver City, Calif.,' and with 'Gladys O'Brien' written on the top left-hand corner. The letter read:

Dear Mr Freed,

I want you to know how very sorry I am I had to take Margaret out of your picture for the time being. She was in bed for a week with a very bad case of hay fever, which the doctor said came from nerves due to overwork, so I am taking her away from everything connected with work for a couple of weeks as I know a change of scenery will do her good. She has been working almost steadily for the past year and a half going from one picture right into another, 'Journey for Margaret', 'You John Jones', 'Dr Gillespe' [*sic*], 'Jane Eyre', 'Lost Angel', 'Madam Curie',

Margaret O'Brien with her mother, Mrs Gladys O'Brien

'Thousands Cheer', 'Canterville Ghost', and now 'Meet Me in St. Louis'.

Even the days she didn't work we still had to make a trip to the studio for publicity interviews, lessons, wardrobe fittings etc, and I was beginning to be greatly criticised for allowing my child to work so hard. We couldn't even take a weekend off because we were always on call, so now we are forced to take a couple of weeks off.

Sincerely

Gladys O'Brien

What film Mrs O'Brien meant by 'You John Jones' earnest study of all available reference books has failed to disclose. Twelve consecutive days were lost, from 31 January to 12 February 1944, a memo stating that the company were 'laying off due to Miss O'Brien's illness'. On 15 February 1944 there was recorded, presumably with a sigh of relief, 'Margaret O'Brien was available for work today.'

At least O'Brien's absence turned out to be limited and precise. Judy Garland caused almost endless problems. When *Meet Me in St. Louis* was being filmed, Garland was only 22 years old. Yet it is clear from her conduct that she was already developing the neurosis that eventually destroyed her career and in the end killed her. She complained, regularly and intermittently, of headaches, migraines, earaches, a bad stomach and the sinus trouble that was popular among several members of the cast. On one occasion she was recorded as having been called for work at 1 p.m. and arriving at 3.15. On another she refused to go on to the set until her hair was bleached, and had to be ordered by Freed to perform. On yet another she telephoned Freed at 4.30 a.m. to say that she might not be able to work ('Lose quarter day account Garland,' said a memo). Another method of procrastination was a telephone call to the studio to warn that her 'car might stall'. That car was a regular source of difficulty: on another occasion the battery ran down and another car had to be sent for her.

Next she complained that she had been up all night with stomach trouble. Another time it was being sleepy rather than wakeful that caused problems: she 'phoned to say she had overslept'. Another time still, she abruptly left the set part-way through shooting. When she did turn up she was often late. Her unreliability caused immense inconvenience, one minute noting: 'Paint down set (sun was not hitting it at time we would have made shot but for Miss Garland's tardiness).' An inter-office communication from David Friedman gives a flavour of the difficulties Garland caused:

> Miss Judy Garland was called today for makeup at 8.30 a.m., on set ready to shoot at 10 a.m. Not having arrived at 9.15, the Assistant Director phoned her at home, and Miss Garland told him she had suffered with earache all night and would be late. She arrived in the studio at 9.49 a.m. and came upon the stage at 10.30 a.m.
>
> During the first shoot Miss Garland was taken ill and excused for ten minutes, then returned and completed the shot.
>
> At lunch time Miss Garland slept with ice packs on her head, removing make-up, hair fall and costume. After lunch Company waited for 35 minutes (1.50 p.m. to 2.25 p.m.) while makeup was renewed, hair re-dressed and costume put on.

Other examples:

| 11.45 to 12.45 | Wait for Judy Garland (Ear requires medical attention consisting of heating oil, pouring it into ear, and laying down for a period). |
| --- | --- |
| 12.30 | Conference – Mr Freed, Mr Minnelli and Miss Garland. |
| | Miss Garland removed wig, make-up and wardrobe and slept thru lunch hour – Nurse called who put icepack on head. |
| | Miss Garland had called Mr Freed to say she had lost her toothbridge – car sent for spare set. |
| | Six takes – director satisfied 3rd but Garland wanted better one. |

Then there are, as samples, two extracts from the daily shooting log. First, 14 February:

> 9.23–10.58 Note – At 9.23 Miss Garland's mother phones Judy was feeling ill but had left for studio anyway. 9.35 arrived thru gate. At 9.55 call came from her dressing room Miss Garland lying down ill and makeup not started. At 10.02 Mr Freed and Mr Friedman went to dressing room. At 10.15 Friedman phoned from dressing room Judy would be on set in 20 minutes – on set 10.50 – getting dressed to 10.58.

Then, on 1 April:

| | |
|---|---|
| 9.55–10.40 | Place people – rehearse and light while waiting for Garland – came thru gate at 9.55. |
| 10.40–11 | Rehearse other principals while waiting for Garland – came on stage at 10.40 – ready 11. |
| 2.20–2.30 | Wait for Garland. |

All told, Judy Garland was away from filming for thirteen days.

What is extraordinary is that there is no trace in the finished film that any of these problems existed. All is smooth and flawless; the continuity is perfect; Judy Garland, beautiful as never before or after, looks as though she has not suffered a moment of pain or discomfort and has slept peacefully for a full eight hours every night.

Shooting continued with, on the night of 3–4 March, a shoot of the Hallowe'en sequence, which started at 8.43 p.m. and, after a 'lunch break' from 11.45 p.m. to 12.45 a.m., ended at 4.55 a.m., with the children kept going with hot soup. Filming was completed and the production closed on 7 April 1944. The songs were recorded, the number then called 'Clang clang clang' being performed at 8.45 p.m. on 1 December 1943 by Judy Garland and a mixed chorus, backed by a 41-man band.

Rows about credits were resolved. Irving Brecher demanded a prominent credit and got one. Lemuel Ayers, fresh from winning acclaim for his sets for the Broadway production of *Oklahoma!*, demanded a special listing. He had to be content with being listed as number two to the Art Director.

The cast received their final payments, at a total cost of $221,500. Judy Garland got $62,500, Mary Astor $19,333.34, Marjorie Main $18,666.67, Joan Carroll $13,666.67, Leon Ames $11,900, Lucille Bremer $6,750, Tom Drake $6,000, and Margaret O'Brien – maybe this was the reason for her mother's recalcitrance – just $5,500. The trolley group between them pocketed $29,666.67. Minnelli's pay was calculated with the utmost precision: 27 weeks pre-production, including $13\frac{2}{6}$ weeks at $500 and $13\frac{4}{6}$ weeks at $1,000, plus 23 weeks production at $1,000 – a total of $43,333.33.

The film was previewed on 5 June and 3 July 1944, and cuts were made. An attempt to excise the Hallowe'en scene, on the grounds that it was too long and held up the action, was resisted by Minnelli and defeated. Less fortunate was the Rodgers and Hammerstein song, 'Boys and Girls Like You and Me'. On 14 July Freed wrote to the composer and lyricist: 'The entire sequence the song was part of was eliminated after the preview on account of its length.'

The final budget was calculated. Filming had lasted seventy days rather than the fifty-eight allotted, and the budget, at $1,707,561.14, was $170,589.21 above what had been allowed for. A reproving pencilled note recorded that 'illnesses plus Margaret O'Brien caused increase'.

The film was released on 31 December. It proved so popular that an MGM lawyer, Bill Danziger, proposed that it should be the first of a series, in the Andy Hardy mould; this idea was fortunately not followed up. It became MGM's most popular film to date, grossing $7,566,000 on its initial release. Sheet music sales of the Trolley Song had, by 21 April 1944, reached the enormous total of 530,227.

*Meet Me in St. Louis* was so successful that other studios tried to imitate it. 20th Century-Fox made *Centennial Summer*, a musical set against the background of the Philadelphia Great Exposition of 1876. Pleasant though it was, the film disappeared without trace. Arthur Freed himself had another go, at MGM, with *Summer Holiday*, an adaptation of Eugene O'Neill's *Ah, Wilderness*. Daringly experimental in technique under the direction of the great Rouben Mamoulian, *Summer Holiday* has survived only as an occasionally revived cult movie.

Despite its great and envied success, *Meet Me in St. Louis* did not win a single Oscar (though Margaret O'Brien's Hallowe'en scene led to her receiving a special Outstanding Child Actress Academy Award). It did, however, attract two serious complaints. A letter from a Methodist minister in Tulsa, Oklahoma, expressed annoyance at the film's alleged concentration on Roman Catholics. And a Mr A. P. Broadfield wrote in from Poughkeepsie, New York:

Gentlemen:

I witnessed the showing of your picture 'Meet Me in St. Louis' and enjoyed it very much.

However, I did see a flaw in the scene in the dining room while having supper, Mr Smith crunched on celery which was of the pascal variety. I do not believe that that particular kind of celery was in existence in 1903.

Thanking you very much for the enjoyment of a really nice picture, I remain

Very truly yours,
A. P. Broadfield

## MINNELLI

Sometimes life can provide bonuses beyond one's wildest imaginings. My early cinemagoing took place in small cinemas in rundown Leeds suburbs, where I would pay 4d (or, in extreme circumstances, 6d) to sit through an evening of transfixing glamour. I did not even conceive of the possibility that I might ever meet anyone involved in the making of the films I saw, especially anyone from the astronomically remote Valhalla of Hollywood. When I watched Gene Kelly in *For Me and My Gal* and, later on, in *Singin' in the Rain*, I never dreamt that the day would come when I would actually meet the man, let alone visit him in his own home in North Rodeo Drive, Beverly Hills, and pore over with him the original shooting script of *Singin' in the Rain*, scorched after its rescue from a fire. Nor did it occur to me that the time would come when I would discuss his films tête-à-tête with Vincente Minnelli.

I saw Minnelli's very first film, *Cabin in the Sky*, when it was released in 1943. I glowed with pleasure at the warm-heartedness of *Meet Me in St. Louis* when in 1945 Minnelli's third film found its way eventually to the Clock Cinema, Roundhay Road, Leeds. Seventeen years later I sat with Minnelli in a plush suite in the Dorchester Hotel, in Park Lane, London, drinking his (or MGM's) tea and discussing with him the filming of *Meet Me in St. Louis*.

By 1962 Minnelli had made twenty-four more films (including *The Four Horsemen of the Apocalypse*, whose British premiere had brought him to London), though in the following fourteen years he was to make only six others (due partly to the decline of the Hollywood studio system and partly to the slump in his own career caused by the flop of *The Four Horsemen of the Apocalypse*, which MGM had forced him to update when he would have preferred to retain its original First World War setting).

Between 1945 and 1962 I had come to idolise Minnelli. I had made it my objective to see all the films of his which I had missed on their first release (including even the strange thriller *Undercurrent*, which featured a Brahms symphony transformed into a piano concerto) and was willing to travel long distances simply to see the mannequin parade from *Lovely to Look At* (a poor remake of *Roberta*), which I had learned Minnelli had directed even though the film as a whole was credited to Mervyn LeRoy.

I never deluded myself that he was a great director, up there in the pantheon with Eisenstein and Renoir. Yet I had come to understand, observe, appreciate and cherish the characteristics which made him so consummately stylish a director, who put a gloss (gloss being, in some circumstances, one of his failings) on everything he touched. His role as director could easily have been discerned from the look of a film even if that film's credits had not climaxed with the words 'Directed by Vincente Minnelli'; words which aroused in me such a tingle, as I anticipated eagerly the opening frame of the film which I had practically run to the cinema to see.

Minnelli was not a great director because he had nothing to say, unlike, for example, Jean Renoir (whose *La Grande Illusion*, Minnelli told me, at our Dorchester meeting, he himself would like to have directed).

In the perfervidly political years of the Hollywood witch-hunts by the House UnAmerican Activities Committee (HUAC), Minnelli, with his then wife Judy Garland, had, to his credit, attended a meeting held at Ira Gershwin's home in Hollywood to oppose the witch-hunts. He had signed a petition expressing 'disgust' at the 'smear' activities of HUAC. He did not, however, join some of the signatories in a subsequent visit to Washington.

When an attempt was made to excise from Minnelli's film *The Bad and the Beautiful* a scene featuring an actor (Ned Glass) who had been blacklisted after falling foul of HUAC, Minnelli fought successfully to retain the scene in the finished picture. His ardour was based not on grounds of political principle but because – as the producer John Houseman remembered – he 'fell in love with the sequence' and could not bear to lose it.

Otherwise, there is little in Minnelli's record to indicate that, apart from his meticulous and fastidious concern with the look of every frame of every film he ever made, he felt strongly about anything. Though reputedly a homosexual himself (though a four times married one), he is not known to have made any particular fuss about the almost total excision of references to homosexuality from the script of the film he directed of the Broadway stage hit *Tea and Sympathy* (whose subject matter dealt with the successful efforts of an older woman to 'cure' a young man of any homosexual propensities he might have had).

However, what I came to admire, and be captivated by, in Minnelli's films was that very concern with the look of every frame and the extraordinary results he thereby achieved. There was in Minnelli's pictures a voluptuousness which could be matched only by Max Ophüls and Luchino Visconti.

As a conversationalist Minnelli was almost inarticulate. Richard Schickel, who interviewed him for his compilation *The Men Who Made the Movies*, said, 'Next to Sir John Gielgud, Vincente Minnelli is the most difficult person I've ever interviewed.' When Minnelli came to London for a *Guardian* lecture at the National Film Theatre, the event was an almost total fiasco because the interviewer could hardly get a coherent sentence out of the eagerly awaited guest. During my conversation with him at the Dorchester, his then (third) wife, a formidable Yugoslav (I think) lady called Denise Giganti, had to act as a kind of interpreter to enable me to get anything out of him. Yet as a movie-maker, as his career both prior to and after *Meet Me in St. Louis* demonstrated, he was dazzlingly eloquent.

Minnelli was certainly not an *auteur*, the sole author of his films, in the way that the French *Cahiers du Cinéma* group of critics believed that a movie director ought to be and often was. In conversation with me, Gene Kelly – himself a director of quality – argued vehemently that the *auteur* theory was baseless because, unlike novels and poems and paintings and sculptures and symphonies which were created by one person alone, a film was the product of a team. Advocates of the *auteur* theory contend that many films endorse the theory: they are concepts of their director, even though the director needs actors, designers, a cinematographer and countless other collaborators (including, most essentially of all, a writer, who is sometimes the director himself) to put the picture on to the screen. François Truffaut, a propagandist for the *auteur* theory, could by this definition himself be regarded as an *auteur*, since his films would not have been made had he not directed them.

Of the films directed by Minnelli, it can be said that only two would not have been made had he not directed them. *Two Weeks in Another Town*, a movie about movie-making, was very consciously undertaken as a successor to Minnelli's *The Bad and the Beautiful*, even containing extracts from that film. *A Matter of Time*, his final movie, was a project launched, nursed and brought to fruition by Minnelli which, even in the butchered state in which it was released, bears all the characteristic signs of its director's craftsmanship. However, even *Lust for Life*, the Van Gogh biography which of all his films was the one which Minnelli most passionately wanted to make, cannot be said to owe its existence to its director. It was an adaptation of a highly popular novel and, even if Minnelli had not directed it, someone else almost certainly would have, even though the outcome could not possibly have been as beautiful and passionate as the Minnelli picture.

For almost his entire career Minnelli worked within the studio system, becoming the longest-serving director at MGM. Being under contract for that studio meant that he had access to all the best talents in Hollywood; it also meant that, in the end, he had to do as he was told: to make films, such as *Kismet* and *The Four Horsemen of the Apocalypse*, which he did not want to make and to make films he did want to make, such as *Brigadoon*, in conditions which he found profoundly unsatisfactory. Whether he liked those conditions or not, like other top-flight Hollywood directors he had to go to work, to clock in and to clock out.

Although *The Wizard of Oz* was credited to Victor Fleming, several other directors worked on it and Fleming himself left the film before it was completed, in order to start work on *Gone with the Wind*, from which George Cukor (who had also done some work on *The Wizard of Oz*) had been removed. Just as other directors took over films (such as *Easter Parade*) intended for Minnelli, so Minnelli took over films (such as *The Clock*) intended for other directors. For *The Clock* he was given sole credit, while for *The Seventh Sin*, which he took over from another director, he did not accept credit. He directed parts of pictures (*Panama Hattie, Lovely to Look At, Till the Clouds Roll By*) which were mainly directed by other men, and he was the main director of *Ziegfeld Follies*, to which other men contributed.

Was Minnelli, then, just a *metteur en scène*, one of countless Hollywood directors who was handed a script and then, with more (in his case) or less (in the case of many others) individuality, put that script on to film? Or was he something more?

The answer is that he was something very much more. It is not simply that his interpolations into the films of others are far superior to the remainder of those movies. The musical numbers he directed for Lena Horne in *Panama Hattie* transcend that dreadful picture. The numbers he directed for Judy Garland in *Till the Clouds Roll By* might have been part of another and far better film; 'Look for the Silver Lining' is especially touching in its expressive simplicity.

All his films, whatever their quality, are immediately recognisable as Minnelli films; they could have been made by no one else. Minnelli was the third director assigned to *The Clock*, but the picture is unquestionably his, with a final audacious boom shot no other director would have imagined, let alone attempted. Moreover, even though each of Minnelli's MGM films was an assignment, he made idiosyncratic and individual contributions to them in all kinds of ways.

Sometimes he would contribute to the script, as he did in *The Band Wagon*, for whose 'Girl Hunt' ballet he wrote the Mickey Spillane pastiche narrative. He interpolated personal jokes and allusions into his movies. On a cinema marquee seen in *The Band Wagon* can be discerned the title 'The Proud Land', the name of *The Bad and the Beautiful*'s film within a film. Minnelli's comedy *The Reluctant Debutante* has the same musical theme as his earlier *Designing Woman*: the director's improvisation during a musicians' strike in Hollywood when *The Reluctant Debutante* was being completed. A Minnelli assignment might, on the face of it, be routine, even banal; but what eventually appeared on the screen, while it might be handicapped by the sheer crassness of the material (as with the absurd melodrama *Undercurrent*), was never routine or banal.

It was for this reason that Minnelli could attract to his films almost every one of the great stars of Hollywood, including not only Garland but Fred Astaire, Gene Kelly, Maurice Chevalier, Judy Holliday, Dean Martin, Barbra Streisand, Yves Montand, Katharine Hepburn, Robert Mitchum, Jennifer Jones, James Mason, Lana Turner, Deborah Kerr, Shirley MacLaine, Frank Sinatra, Edward G. Robinson, Richard Burton, Elizabeth Taylor, Liza Minnelli, Ingrid Bergman, Lucille Ball, Lauren Bacall, Gregory Peck, Rex Harrison, Kirk Douglas (his favourite) and Spencer Tracy (his second favourite). John Wayne, Minnelli told me, had a standing joke that they should make a Western together (although it was with Mitchum that Minnelli made his sole Western, *Home from the Hill*).

While Minnelli was best known for his musicals – and rightly, because he was by far the greatest director of musicals there has ever been, with only Stanley Donen and Gene Kelly fit to compare with him – nearly two-thirds of his output consisted of comedies, romantic dramas and melodramas. He was able to find an appropriate style for each one, from the *noir* brooding of *The Bad and the Beautiful* to the consummately successful slapstick of the too-little-revived comedy he made with Lucille Ball and Desi Arnaz about the vicissitudes of life in a mobile home, *The Long Long Trailer*.

By the time he left MGM Minnelli had become the longest-serving director employed by the studio. It was Paramount that first lured him to Hollywood; but, although in the end it was Paramount which sponsored the last of his films that was released more or less as he wanted it, *On a Clear Day You Can See Forever*, he was originally so dissatisfied with their treatment of him that he bought out his first Hollywood contract and returned to New York, where he was a highly admired director of stage extravaganzas, at the gigantic Radio City Music Hall and elsewhere.

However, it was at MGM that he really found his niche because, although this plush company played safe in its subject matter (unlike the socially conscious Warner Bros), it was in its opulence the natural home for the luxurious *mise-en-scène* in which Minnelli basked and sometimes wallowed. Furthermore, the special self-contained unit created by Louis B. Mayer for Arthur Freed was particularly hospitable to the kind of offbeat talent of which Minnelli was an exemplar. If Minnelli flourished in the environment created by Freed, he also helped that environment to burgeon.

*Meet Me in St. Louis*, which was Freed's special baby and in the end turned out even more to be Minnelli's, was so great a success that from then on Mayer felt unable to deny Freed anything. We can, indeed, thank Minnelli for one of the tiny handful of MGM musicals that was better than anything Minnelli himself ever made. When Freed, a song-writer in partnership with Nacio Herb Brown before he became a movie-maker, went to Mayer and asked why MGM could not buy up his own song catalogue just as other studios were buying up other writers' catalogues, Mayer (so Stanley Donen once told me when I visited him at his mansion in Bel Air) so loved Freed that he decided to purchase his catalogue as a way of giving his surrogate son a capital gain. It was this catalogue, now an MGM property, which Freed handed to the scriptwriters Betty Comden and Adolph Green with the instructions that they should choose whatever songs they wished from it and include them in a film which, he stipulated, must be named after one of those songs, 'Singin' in the Rain'.

Freed was not Minnelli's only producer. Another was John Houseman, an estranged associate of Orson Welles, with whom he had created the astonishing Mercury Theatre in Manhattan. Houseman was brought to MGM by Mayer's successor as head of production, Dore Schary, and made it possible for Minnelli to direct one of his special gems, *The Bad and the Beautiful*, and his most cherished project, *Lust for Life*, the biography of Van Gogh (both of these, far from coincidentally, being essays about the rewards and hazards of the artistic process).

As his experience of directing different kinds of film accumulated, Minnelli became a cinematic virtuoso. Some directors are noted for the composition of their frames. Some are masters of movement within the frame. Some have particular talent for directing actors. Some are masters of colour. Some, though not many, have a particular ability to stage a musical number. In every one of these departments, Minnelli was easily as good as the very best. Furthermore, there were two aspects of filling out a frame and giving it life where Minnelli was out on his own far beyond any rival; and one additional area that was all Minnelli's own.

A vintage example of composition within the frame was the prince's procession in the musical *Kismet*, a film which Minnelli himself had not liked at all (he told me that operetta was not his metier) but to which he had given his best shot all the same. The procession was prolonged and complex; but that was not enough for Minnelli. It had, as well, to be reflected perfectly in a pool which the procession passed.

Ostentation was one form at which Minnelli excelled. Another was the tension and menace brought about by the obscurity of chiaroscuro. When, in *The Bad and the Beautiful*, Kirk Douglas as the soon-to-be-lover and film producer of Georgia Lorison (Lana Turner) comes looking for her in the shadowy house of her recently dead father, a doppelgänger for John Barrymore, he enters a room plunged in shadow, with the ominous voice of the dead Lorison senior (spoken by Louis Calhern) delivering the 'Tomorrow and tomorrow' speech from *Macbeth*. All is in shadow, and out of the shadows comes Georgia's drunken voice.

For movement within the frame notable examples are so numerous as to make choice difficult. There is the incredible crane shot, the camera rising higher and higher from the singer to take in the panorama almost of a whole neighbourhood, in the ''S Wonderful' number from *An American in Paris*. In the opening number of *Gigi*, 'Thank Heaven for Little Girls', the camera does the opposite, lurching into the frame to drag the spectator into a children's game. In *The Band Wagon*, during the reading of a script for potential backers, the camera slots different groups together with such complexity that the solution to Rubik's cube would be easier to work out. For the viewer, however, the action is deceptively simple. In the 'Bored' number from *Kismet* the camera is a participant in the choreography, weaving towards and around Dolores Gray's undulating body. In *Designing Woman* the camera tracks gradually and relentlessly across a room to focus on a conversation between Gregory Peck and Lauren Bacall.

The staging by Minnelli of musical numbers makes most other directors of musicals look like tyros. 'Drop That Name' in *Bells Are Ringing* starts with participants milling at random and ends with them, having almost imperceptibly moved to their positions, marshalled in parading ranks. In the 'Nina' number in *The Pirate* there is a marvel of movement as Gene Kelly, an acrobat who becomes mistaken for a Caribbean buccaneer, swings from building to building, encountering beautiful women on the way. *Brigadoon* implicates the swirl of bagpipes into the number 'Come Home with Bonnie Jean' (which had to be restaged after Minnelli, a stickler for accuracy, had incautiously instructed the Highland dancers to wear nothing underneath their kilts and had been confronted with a censorable outcome). In *Gigi*, Louis Jourdan is photographed in silhouette, based on the caricatures of the artist Sem, as he sings the title number.

Yet Minnelli can be at his most effective when at his most simple. In *An American in Paris* he just sets back the camera and lets us watch Kelly tap-dancing in 'I Got Rhythm', and he captures the melancholy of burgeoning love in the number 'Love is Here to Stay', sung and danced by Kelly and Leslie Caron on a Seine embankment. The same kind of getting-to-know-you emotions are depicted in the equally straightforward, yet choreographically sublime, 'Dancing in the Dark', performed in *The Band Wagon* by Fred Astaire and Cyd Charisse (whom this film made a major star) in a sequence which Gene Kelly once told me he regarded as the best dance number ever filmed.

In the ball sequence of *Madame Bovary*, which begins intoxicatingly and ends feverishly, the camera swirls among the dancers. In the final, intensely moving, sequence of *The Clock*, the camera in the concourse of Pennsylvania station in New York moves up and up and up from the separating couple of Judy Garland and Robert Walker, who have met, fallen in love, lost each other, found each other, married and then parted when he goes to war, all in the space of a day. The two are lost from view among a vast crowd, in a technically masterly shot which is not gratuitous but tells us that this is just one story and that, among all the other unidentifiable people we now see, there may be many more special stories.

All but eight of Minnelli's pictures were made in colour. In each one he found new ways of astounding the viewer. When, in *An American in Paris*, the artist Jerry Mulligan (Kelly) begins preparing for his exhibition, the first image in the montage sequence is an astounding frame of a painter's vivid palette. The market-place sequence in *Kismet* is dominated by swirling cloths of vivid hues. *On a Clear Day You Can*

*See Forever* opens with shots of buds burgeoning into gorgeously coloured flowers, under the telepathic Barbra Streisand's green fingers.

Minnelli was unique in the use of decor. He had been a window-dresser at Marshall Fields' store in Chicago and then a set-designer at Radio City Music Hall in New York. He knew better than almost anyone else how to dress a set and was fastidious to the point of pernicketiness in choosing just the right objects. *Gigi*, with its ornate and opulent Paris interiors, is a prize example of what he could do.

Minnelli was unique in the deployment of extras. Other directors used extras to populate the sets as living, but still almost inanimate, dummies. Minnelli turned them into real people. *The Clock* was a simple story, and Minnelli kept it simple. Having taken over the assignment of directing this little black-and-white picture after another director had been removed from it, he decided that every one of the extras should have a life of his or her own, and be a character, not a cipher. So each of them was given something specific to do and to be: what Minnelli described to me in our Dorchester meeting as 'bits of character'. Soon he became known in the trade as 'extra-crazy'.

In later films Minnelli had a particular partiality for peopling New York scenes with individualistic, even eccentric, people. *Bells Are Ringing* provides an excellent example, with extras first being presented as monstrous and distorted and then as friendly and harmless. An exceptional specimen is the New York cocktail bar scene from *Brigadoon*. Kelly, back from the Scottish Highlands where he has found and then lost his 'dearie', Cyd Charisse, meets his American fiancée. They are surrounded by gesticulating, gossiping individuals in a dazzling sequence which the *New Yorker*'s film critic, Pauline Kael, said came as a great relief from all those grinning men in tartan (with or without underwear).

More idiosyncratic to Minnelli's style than any other part of his work were what came to be known as the 'bizarre' sequences, of which there was at least one (and sometimes more than one) in each of his films. These were lurid, feverish episodes, unrealistic in nature and full of swirling colour and action. Often they were chases, as in a pursuit through a fairground in *Some Came Running* and the race to head off the man whose escape will destroy the village of Brigadoon. In *Father of the Bride* the bizarre sequence was a neurotic nightmare as Spencer Tracy, hating the preparations for his daughter's wedding, dreams in advance of the humiliation he is sure he will suffer. In *Home from the Hill* there is a terrifying boar hunt. In some of Minnelli's musicals the bizarre sequences are prolonged ballets: in *An American in Paris*, the climactic denouement involving a forlorn Kelly, who believes he has lost Leslie Caron for good, and featuring mini-episodes in which famous fin-de-siècle paintings are animated; in *The Band Wagon*, a send-up of Mickey Spillane in the 'Girl Hunt' sequence, whose parodistic commentary Minnelli wrote himself.

Most remarkable of all, and one of the most hysterical episodes in all movies, is a car drive involving Lana Turner in *The Bad and the Beautiful*. Rushing away from the producer Jonathan Shields' house, where she has found him with a scornful 'other woman' (the marvellous Elaine Stewart – Kelly's New York fiancée in *Brigadoon* – draped over the bannisters), Turner gets into her car and drives away at breakneck speed, with rain beating at the window as she screams and howls in a paroxysm of uncontrolled grief. On paper it was nothing. On screen it was devastating.

An anthology of key sequences in Minnelli films would provide some of the most remarkable moments in all cinema. Probably, among Hollywood directors, only John Ford and Alfred Hitchcock could come up with competing compendiums, and even they would fall short through absence of musical numbers. Even so, the Minnelli treasury is incomplete. Contractual difficulties prevented him from being able to direct the film version of *My Fair Lady* which, in his hands, must certainly have been far better than George Cukor's pedestrian version. A long-standing MGM project for Minnelli to direct *Say It With Music*, a film devoted to Irving Berlin numbers, was after much preparation aborted because Berlin was unable to supply the required new songs. Another Berlin project which did get made, *Easter Parade*, was to have been directed by Minnelli until Judy Garland, by now estranged from him, vetoed his participation. Minnelli could not have helped providing a better version than the dull entertainment – except for 'A Couple of Swells' – that the less stylish Charles Walters supplied.

Vincente Minnelli had not at first been intended to direct *Meet Me in St. Louis*. The director scheduled to make the film was George Cukor, who was highly experienced, having begun his directing career in 1930 and been entrusted with some of MGM's most prestigious projects. He was particularly favoured by Garbo (as in *Camille*). As *Little Women* had already shown and as *The Actress* was later to show again, he had a deft touch with cosy, family-based nostalgia. Sally Benson had written contentedly to Cukor, 'I am terribly glad you are the one for Kensington.' Then Cukor went into the army, and so lost the chance to make what turned out to be one of the most cherished movies ever filmed. Years later he was to have his revenge, by winning the assignment on which Minnelli had set his heart, the screen version of *My Fair Lady*.

*Meet Me in St. Louis* was of course filmed before all of Minnelli's increasingly accomplished later successes, but all these later films are foreshadowed in it. Before it, Minnelli had directed only two complete pictures. The first was a relatively small-scale musical, *Cabin in the Sky*, which was a specialised item in that it had an all-black cast. Minnelli gave the film an unusual look by photographing it not in black and white but in sepia. *Cabin in the Sky* was a great success but, by its nature, a one-off. Then came a ghastly comedy, *I Dood It*, in which Minnelli's journeyman assignment was not to produce a work of art but to turn out a vehicle for the then hugely (now, inexplicably) popular comedian Red Skelton.

So now Arthur Freed was putting this new and almost untried director in charge of a lush musical featuring one of the studio's top, highly temperamental and in this case extremely reluctant stars, Judy Garland. There was to be a large budget. The movie was to be filmed in the then far from universal Technicolor process. What is more, this was a picture in which most high-ups in the studio had no confidence. The studio head had to be talked into making it, and the whole endeavour was written off in advance, as a potential folly, an indulgence for Freed. It is important to remember that, although today we can only think of *Meet Me in St. Louis* as we now know it, in 1944 no one at MGM had any idea of how the completed project would turn out. It could have been a routine product, a bore, a flop.

Minnelli wrote years later, in his ghosted memoirs *I Remember It Well*: 'After Arthur's string of successes, the studio owed him a failure.' Yet if it was Freed who invented the concept of the picture and got it into production, it was Minnelli alone who believed in all of it and believed in it throughout. First, Minnelli had to talk a heel-dragging Garland (whom he hardly knew) into making the film. Then, with an overall concept glowing in his mind and his alone, he set out, sequence by sequence and sometimes frame by frame, to make the picture uniquely his. He took enormous – and, to fellow-participants, sometimes infuriating – trouble composing the frames so that each one, if frozen, would be a work of art. A former window-dresser, he regarded the apt placement of almost unobtrusive objects as essential. One daily report of the filming recorded, '3.20–3.26 Wait for perfume bottle (special container with satin lining asked for by director).'

Minnelli believed that the texture of a movie depended on immense care over details which the audience might not even notice consciously. He said of the making of *Meet Me in St. Louis*, 'You have to have great discipline in what you do. I spent a great deal of time in research, and finding the right things for it. I feel that a picture that stays with you is made up of a hundred or more hidden things.'

Minnelli was fastidious about each costume item that helped perfect a character's personality. The red Tam o' Shanter worn by Katie, the maid, and which helped give her her rakish character, was inspired by an item of headgear sported by Minnelli's spinster aunt Anna. The look of the film had to have its own special period style. Minnelli decided it 'should have the look of Thomas Eakins' paintings, though not to the point of imitation'. Each of the picture's four seasonal

Katie in her red Tam o' Shanter

segments would be introduced by a shot of the Smiths' American Gothic house as a filigreed illustration, like a greetings card of the period. Each card, first seen in monochrome, blushed into colour and then burst into life and action.

The trouble to which Minnelli went in composing a scene can be judged from the following extract from a daily report:

1 April 1944

4.18–5.02   Clear set – extend it (stairs – shrubs etc), build track from long pullaway shot with double screen fade out of picture.

5.02–5.22   Rehearse camera pull back with stand-ins and process on – meanwhile move Buffalo Statue to opposite side of set.

5.22–5.45   Director discusses other angles trying same with finder for pull back with camera, process camera and art director.

5.45–6.00   Rehearse original angle with standins and people before process.

6.00–7.00   Dismiss people – director orders buffalo returned to 1st position – director felt buffalo could be used to frame finale of fadeout but decided instead to use fountain for finale if it were moved closer to terrace and process screens. Considerable discussion as to feasibility of this move, and it was decided to move the fountain over the week-end, thus providing the frame the director felt he needs to complete the shot.

Staff and crew dismissed: 7.00.


Audiences never did get to see that buffalo, but the buffalo had its chance for 98 minutes of Minnellian cogitation.

Camera movement in *Meet Me in St. Louis* is meticulous and often voluptuous. One piece of movement is, so far as I am aware, unique in all cinema. In many films it is almost a cliché for a camera to sail up to a window and peek in. Sometimes, after a cut, the camera will move into the room beyond the window. In the Christmas ball scene in *Meet Me in St. Louis* the camera sails – or appears to do so – not only up to but right

43

4 4   The camera sails through the window

through what is clearly a solid window. I asked Minnelli how this apparent miracle had been accomplished, and he told me that the set was built in two imperceptibly dovetailed parts, meeting at the window. When the camera reached the window the two parts of the set were separated to allow the camera to sail through. An eagle-eyed spectator, tipped off in advance, can just spot the split as it happens.

That move was complex in concept but simple in realisation. Another shot was extraordinarily complex in execution. This is the scene in which Esther and John Truett go around the Smith house turning out the ceiling lights one by one in order to provide the appropriate setting for what Esther hopes (in vain) will result in a goodnight kiss. Minnelli decided he wanted to film this scene in one shot, the camera moving non-stop from light to light. The set-up was dizzyingly intricate, and the lighting cameraman, George Folsey, later recalled this sequence – which took four days to light and rehearse – as the most difficult thing he ever had to do. Originally the scene contained five pages of dialogue, but Minnelli decided that all this talk held up the action, and junked all five pages. Instead he substituted camera movement. A whole day was spent in rehearsal, but the actual filming was achieved immediately the next morning's work began.

Minnelli's direction of featured actors extended from thinking up small bits of business that filled out their characters to a carefully conceptual approach to whole scenes. Small but beguiling touches include a charming moment during Rose's telephone conversation with Warren Sheffield. Mrs Smith, at the rear of the set, moves to close the window to prevent the neighbours from overhearing. Another lovely notion enhances the scene where the family, following Mr Smith's revelation that they are going to have to move to New York, reassemble to listen to their father singing to their mother's piano accompaniment. They had been eating cake when shocked by the announcement of the forthcoming disruption of their lives. Now they once again pick up their plates with the slices of cake. Tootie, sitting on Esther's lap, tries to filch a bit of her sister's cake. Esther foils Tootie's move, and then feeds her a morsel of cake on her fork. The sense of sisterly love is almost tangible.

Minnelli took enormous care with the big scenes. Dissatisfied with the screenplay as it stood for the scene of John Truett's proposal to Esther towards the end of the film, he discussed with one of the

4 6    Esther and John Truett turning out the lights

scriptwriters (Irving Brecher, Finklehoffe having left to work on a play), how the episode could be improved. Still unhappy with what he had, he decided to write the scene himself. The scene as he filmed it was fashioned into a perfect encapsulation of the fluctuating emotions of two young people in love. They agree to marry, they assert that the family's departure to New York will not part them; and then they accept that their parting is inevitable.

Minnelli took special care with the scene that followed, in which Tootie, distraught that she will have to abandon her snowmen when she leaves for New York, decides to smash them. The daily report describes how the scene was prepared.

| | |
|---|---|
| 11.15–11.28 | Clear set for high shot – take camera to porch roof. |
| 11.28–12.35 | Line and light 4th setup – shot of snow people in moonlight. Effects and change from day to nite nighting [*sic*]. |
| 12.35–12.36 | Shoot 1 take. |
| 12.36–12.40 | Pick 5th setup. |
| | Lunch 12.40–1.40. 1 hour. |
| 1.40–2.00 | Rehearse mechanics of scene – (Margaret smashing snow people) and pick setup. |
| 2.00–2.20 | Line and light. |
| 2.20–2.32 | Rehearse Judy and Margaret. |
| 2.32–2.46 | Reset snow people for action as rehearsed – continue line and light. |
| 2.46–3.20 | Saw snow people for smashing. |
| 3.20–3.55 | Rehearse and check up light on positions while rehearsing. |
| 3.55–4.00 | Fix Judy's hair and make-up while trimming arcs. |
| 4.00–4.08 | Final rehearsal and time out for Margaret to cry. |
| 4.08–4.09 | Shoot – 1 take. |

| 4.09–4.10 | Stills – Production and set. |
| 4.10–4.20 | Decide to shoot roof angle first before snow people fall apart. |
| 4.20–4.45 | Rehearse and line and light 6th set-up while rehearsing. |
| 4.45–4.51 | Time out for Margaret to cry. |
| 4.51–4.52 | Shoot – 1 take. |
| 4.52–5.12 | Line and light 7th setup. |
| 5.12–5.23 | Rehearse. |
| 5.23–5.30 | Check up light. |
| 5.30–5.37 | Margaret getting ready to cry. |
| 5.37–5.43 | Shoot – 3 takes. |
| 5.43–5.45 | Still. |
| | Dismissed 5.45. |

Behind these bald logistics, though, was concealed the process of getting Tootie (six-year-old Margaret O'Brien) to cry. Histrionics of

Mrs Smith closes the window while Rose is on the telephone with Warren

this kind had in previous films been stimulated, usually, by the child's mother and/or aunt. On this occasion, Mrs O'Brien had had a falling-out with Margaret and told Minnelli that it was up to him to get her daughter to shed tears. She advised Minnelli that he would have to upset Margaret deeply and this he proceeded to do, describing to her in the most bloodthirsty terms the shooting to death of her dog. The tears came. Three takes (not the one take remembered by Minnelli in his memoirs) were made for safety's sake. Margaret, Minnelli recalled, then skipped happily off the set while he went home feeling like a monster.

One extraordinary moment, in which acting was combined with action to provide a remarkable cinematic effect, comes when an unnoticed Mr Smith has seen, through an upstairs window, Tootie's smashing of the snowmen. He walks downstairs, sits in his usual armchair, and gets out a match to light his usual cigar. The lighting of the match illuminates the whole screen, and its flame is simultaneous with, and symbolic of, Smith's change of mind: the family will stay in St. Louis. Seven years later Minnelli would use a comparable effect, again involving smoking, in *An American in Paris*. Gene Kelly (Jerry) and Leslie Caron (Lisa) are making tearful and final farewells; their love has no future because of Caron's feeling of obligation to Henri

Esther feeds Tootie cake

(Georges Guetary). From a carefully positioned camera angle we see a plume of smoke. Guetary is then revealed as the smoker. He has, unseen, overheard the anguish of his lover and, after the dream ballet, he will give up Lisa to Jerry.

With *Meet Me in St. Louis*, Minnelli was directing his first colour film. Yet he was not scared of challenging the Technicolor supervisor, Natalie Kalmus. This formidable and feared lady forbade Minnelli to clothe one sister in bright red and another in bright green, warning that a clash between these two hues would cause the camera to pick them up as rust and greenish black. Minnelli ignored her, and was proved right.

Minnelli, indeed, had a colour scheme for the whole film, as described in *Vincente Minnelli and the Film Musical* by Joseph Andrew Casper, published in 1977:

> *St. Louis'* four seasons are designated by specific colours – summer's reds and roses, autumn's oranges, yellows, browns, winter's deep blues and fuscous, and spring's white. The darkening of the values parallels the dimming of the family's hope of attending the fair. When all seems lost, the colour is drained from the frame. Mr Smith, in an ebony smoking jacket,

Mr Smith lights his cigar

leaves the window from which he witnessed Tootie's destruction of the snowmen in the black night. He rambles through Agnes' bedroom in darkness, descends the step to the parlour, and comes to rest in an indigo chair. Brown barrels of paper-wrapped objects line jagged shadows across the room. Even the walls have a square area, lighter than the rest, where colourful pictures used to hang. He strikes a match to light a cigar and keeps an orange flame burning, suggestive of the light in his head or idea (the use of the prop as dramatic point). The camera dollies in and the scene suddenly is suffused with light and warmth. The flame burns his fingers. He shouts, 'Anna', rises and turns up the desk lamp. The family in variously hued frocks resembles a crazy quilt on the steps. Gramps turns up the gas jets. The climax comes when the Smith family is assured of being in St. Louis for the fair and colour rushes through the house like blood through a once-frozen body. The dazzling white of the next sequence denotes newness and renovation.

Minnelli brought a special, individual touch to the song sequences. The Trolley Song was written by Martin and Blane, very reluctantly, at Freed's insistence. Unlike its marvellous counterpart in *The Harvey Girls*, 'On the Atchison, Topeka and the Santa Fe', which is a huge production number, the Trolley Song is simple and intimate in concept though depending on complex editing to link the shots.

The structure of the Trolley Song number was not designed to fit the trolley car. The trolley car was designed, and specially built, to suit the needs of the number. One of the film's art directors, Jack Martin Smith, told Hugh Fordin for his book *The World of Entertainment!*:

I designed the trolley with the aisles wide enough so people could pass up and down. We made the ceilings high enough so that they could be lighted. We constructed the winding staircase so that it could accommodate people and also hold down the weight of all the dancers running back and forth, up and down, in their costumes, so that they could hang out the windows, which people don't do on a real streetcar. ... We started the trolley running and it had to go for several blocks. We had to have several angles; straight side, three-fourth back, one fourth front.

Despite all these complexities, the number as seen on film flows and bubbles with the zest and pace of apparent inevitability.

Moreover, Minnelli decided to turn this scene from a delightful, uncomplicated song, performed by Garland and a chorus, into a plot point with tension. Will John Truett get away from basketball practice in time to catch the trolley? Minnelli makes the audience as anxious as Esther, first by making us aware of Esther's despair at John's absence, then by showing him running desperately to catch the trolley. The sight of his strenuous efforts to keep a date with Esther transforms the scene into one of exhilaration, the high spirits of the song enhanced by Esther's personal happiness.

A mood of touching nostalgia was created by Minnelli's handling of the song 'You and I', in which Mr and Mrs Smith assert their inseparability based on their shared experiences. A singing voice for Leon Ames, as Mr Smith, had to be dubbed; but Minnelli did not want a professional singer. Instead he asked the writer of the lyric, the producer of the film, Arthur Freed himself, to sing the song. Freed loved doing it, in what Minnelli described as a 'sweet croak'.

Minnelli added another personal touch, which was also the perfect touch, to the wistful song 'Have Yourself a Merry Little

'Have Yourself a Merry Little Christmas'

Christmas', which Esther sings consolingly, but unavailingly, to Tootie before she rushes out to smash the snowmen. Minnelli had found a music box with a monkey on it in an antique toy shop in New York. He made it the touching centrepiece of Esther's attempted comforting of Tootie.

Although it was in his next film, *The Clock*, that Minnelli's extra-craziness first manifested itself substantially, the tendency was already there right at the start of *Meet Me in St. Louis*. As the first of the filigreed greetings cards come to life, a beer wagon rolls by with a group of boys larking about on it. The handling of the small children in the Hallowe'en sequence is an even more vivid example of the way in which Minnelli gave individuality to minor characters with tiny roles.

The Hallowe'en sequence is one of the few substantial episodes transferred from the Sally Benson book (though in the book Agnes rather than Tootie is the chief character, because Agnes was Sally Benson). Minnelli claimed that the Hallowe'en sequence was the principal reason he did the film. For the children's costumes he raided the MGM wardrobe in exactly the way that the children would have raided their own attics. The scene was filmed at night-time and into the early hours of 4 March 1944. The cameras rolled from 8.43 p.m. until

The Hallowe'en sequence

11 p.m., at which point – an example of Minnelli's perfectionism – there was a pause until 11.32 p.m. to discuss 'change in setup to give more eerie effect'. Then came a 'lunch' break from 11.45 p.m. to 12.45 a.m. The seven hours of shooting finished at 4.55 a.m.

Minnelli was very happy with the completed sequence, but Freed feared that its inclusion slowed down the film's pace. He was with great difficulty, and some acrimony, persuaded to keep the sequence in the film for the first preview, after a private studio screening without it. 'I was dying,' recalled Minnelli. But he won. When the lights came up, Freed admitted, 'It's not the same picture. Let's put it back.' Not only was the Hallowe'en sequence a bewitching element in the completed film; it was the first of the bizarre sequences which were from then on to feature in the director's work throughout his career.

If *Meet Me in St. Louis* consolidated Freed's power at MGM, it established Minnelli once, for all, and permanently, as a top MGM director with a particular talent for directing musicals. His eventual oeuvre included *An American in Paris*, which won the best picture Oscar, and *Gigi* which, in addition to the best picture Oscar, won Minnelli the Oscar for best director. He has a fair claim to be regarded as the greatest director of musicals in the history of the cinema. Of all his musicals, the one nearest to perfection, and the one most regularly revived, is undoubtedly *Meet Me in St. Louis*.

## JUDY

There she sat at the edge of the stage, her feet dangling into the orchestra pit. No star this century has carried with her the emotional baggage that weighed down Judy Garland.

I had seen other great artists perform, in London theatres and elsewhere. Ethel Merman was entirely uncomplicated, simply belting out the numbers that she had made famous and that had made her famous. Shirley MacLaine sang and danced, and even her nonsensical pseudo-philosophical musing failed to get in the way of her superb accomplishments as an entertainer. Eartha Kitt made it clear that no external circumstances would be permitted to come between her and her dominance of the audience. But Judy Garland at the Dominion in London was surrounded, almost as if it were ectoplasm, by her redolent past both on-screen and off.

Arthur Freed

It is remarkable how few of the greatest screen legends have appeared in more than a couple of films of exceptional quality. Garbo glowed in many movies, but no more than three of them – *Queen Christina, Camille, Ninotchka* – stand up as anything more than vehicles for her magic. Gable? Cite *It Happened One Night* and *Gone with the Wind*, and most of the rest is dross. Marilyn Monroe remained an icon more than thirty years after her death. Yet while two of the films in which she had bit-parts (*The Asphalt Jungle* and *All About Eve*) are classics, of the movies in which she starred only *Some Like it Hot* and *The Seven Year Itch* are really worth reviving on their intrinsic merits.

Look at Judy Garland's movies, and pain accompanies pleasure. 'Dear Mr Gable', the birthday present that Roger Edens wrote for her to sing for Clark at his MGM birthday party and which she then repeated

in a featured spot in *Broadway Melody of 1938*, was the number which singled her out from the crowd and set her on the road which ended in a drugged death at the age of 47. 'Get Happy' was the number which, though tremendous as a solo item, stood out in *Summer Stock* as the sequence in which the slimmed-down, apparently joyous Judy seemed a completely different person from the sad, plump, puffy-faced woman who inhabited the rest of the film. *A Star is Born*, brilliant in its hysterical way, is remembered as the butchered comeback that did not work. *Gay Purr-ee* was the descent to rock-bottom, as a soundtrack voice for a cartoon character, of the woman Gene Kelly told me was the greatest entertainer he had ever known.

Of all the musicals that Garland made, only two are as near-perfect as dammit. One, *The Wizard of Oz*, is affecting to watch on one level for its innocence, and painful on a different level for the retrospective knowledge of what became of that innocence. Though Garland's presence made it extra-special, it was not designed for her. She was only cast because 20th Century-Fox would not loan out Shirley Temple to MGM. *Meet Me in St. Louis* is not only easily the best musical that Garland ever made, immaculate in its perfection; it is the only Garland musical which can be viewed without any pangs, which is entirely unconnected with any extraneous event (except her burgeoning love affair with its director) and a joy to watch. Not a single shadow, of the past or the future, darkens that joy. It is paradoxical that this is the film Judy Garland simply did not want to make.

Her lover of that time, the screenwriter and future director Joseph Mankiewicz, told her that, at the age of 22, for her to play a teenager again, after she had been cast in an adult role in the preceding *Presenting Lily Mars*, would be a step backward. Who today remembers *Presenting Lily Mars* (pleasant and clever film though it was)? Who today can forget *Meet Me in St. Louis*?

Garland's career, in retrospect, can be seen to be divided in two sections: before and after *Meet Me in St. Louis*. Before *Meet Me in St. Louis* she had never made a film which was fashioned as a vehicle solely for her. Most of her previous movies had been intended as Mickey Rooney–Judy Garland vehicles (*Thoroughbreds Don't Cry*, the Andy Hardy series, *Babes in Arms*, *Babes on Broadway*, *Strike Up the Band*, *Girl Crazy*) with Rooney much the bigger star. In *Little Nellie Kelly* and *For Me and My Gal* she had co-stars (George Murphy in the first, Gene Kelly in the second). *Presenting Lily Mars*, of which she was rightly so proud, had originally been intended for Lana Turner. Subsequently Kathryn Grayson was considered for the role before Garland was cast to co-star with Van Heflin.

*Meet Me in St. Louis* was Garland's first film entirely in colour; the first to have a screenplay written especially around her by a writer (Fred Finklehoffe) especially committed to her; the first to have a collection of new songs written specially for her; and the first in which – with two exceptions ('I Was Drunk Last Night', sung by Margaret O'Brien, and 'You and I', sung by D. Markas and Arthur Freed) – all the numbers either were sung by her alone or included her among the singers. It was the first film in which she established a smash hit of the time (the Trolley Song) and only the second in which she sang a song, written especially for her, which has lasted half a century ('Have Yourself a Merry Little Christmas' – the other being 'Over the Rainbow'). 'Have Yourself a Merry Little Christmas' is, however, different from 'Over the Rainbow' in having a life independent of its original singer and of the context in which it was sung, even though its lyric was rewritten specifically to suit the wishes of that singer, Garland.

The success of *Meet Me in St. Louis* provided Garland not only with increased affection from the public, who already loved her, but for the first time with huge clout within the studio. Her glowing performance gave her the chance to make her only non-musical at MGM, the exquisite and touching *The Clock*, in which she showed herself to be a superb actress even when not buttressed by the songs she could perform better than anyone else before or since. It ensured that never again at MGM did she make a black-and-white musical. It was the first film she was trusted to carry without a male star alongside her (Van Johnson having been replaced by the far less well-known, even though perfectly suitable, Tom Drake). It was the first film in which the make-up was devised not to disguise her but to enhance her. It was the film which, making more money than any MGM movie ever had before, showed her to be indispensable to the studio, and so bestowed upon her power she had never had before; power which she used ruthlessly both while the film was being made and ever afterwards; power which was to lead first to her dismissal by MGM, then to her ruin, and eventually to her death.

Never again was she to make a film of so immaculate a quality. *The Pirate*, though it had marvellous moments and a superb atmosphere, did not really come off; *Easter Parade*, which might have been far better if she had not forced Minnelli to be removed from it, was a pleasant enough confection but is remembered today only for one sublime number, 'A Couple of Swells'. By establishing her for the first time as an unchallenged superstar, *Meet Me in St. Louis* created three apparently contradictory and successive personas for Garland: the idol of tens of millions of loyal fans; the icon of a cult; the mascot of a camp following. *Meet Me in St. Louis* provided the impetus from which the whole of the rest of Judy Garland's life followed. If she had not made it her life might have been entirely different. She might not have married Vincente Minnelli, with whom she began an affair during the making of the film. She would, therefore, not have given birth to Liza Minnelli. She might not have misbehaved as she did during the shooting of *Meet Me in St. Louis* and as she increasingly went on to do. She might have lived longer than forty-seven years.

It was not only Mankiewicz who almost prevented her from following along what now seems to have been a pre-ordained path. Louis B. Mayer, the head of MGM, agreed with Garland that *Meet Me in*

*St. Louis* was unsuitable for her, and gave her permission not to make it. Arthur Freed persisted in his wish for her to star in it; but it was Minnelli who in the end persuaded her; remarkably so, since at the time they hardly knew one another and, as a director of only two movies to date, he had little standing at MGM.

Minnelli records in his memoirs how Garland came to see him about the film. 'She looked at me as if we were planning an armed robbery against the American public. She later told me that she'd come to see me thinking I would see it her way.' Minnelli recollects that Garland said to him, 'It's not very good, is it?' It had, in fact, before the final shooting script truly been unsatisfactory, with Esther enmeshed in several romances and beset by a blackmail plot; but those faults had been remedied. Minnelli replied, 'I think it's fine. I see a lot of great things in it. In fact, it's magical.' After Mayer upheld Garland's objections and Freed insisted on overriding them, Garland reluctantly gave way.

However, at first she participated with ill grace. She mocked Minnelli off-screen and, unlike Lucille Bremer, who as the oldest sister Rose acted with committed sincerity, she mocked the lines she had to speak on the set. Minnelli's intricate set-ups meant that rehearsals were needed before shooting, and Garland tried to dodge these, racing off in her car and having to be intercepted at the studio gate. In the end it was a telling-off by Mary Astor – who, indeed, gave Garland a piece of her mind on more than one occasion – that caused her to change her attitude.

Another change of attitude resulted from the approach of the make-up woman allocated to her. In her earlier films, Garland had long been routinely equipped with rubber discs to change the shape of her nose and caps to disguise her slightly irregular teeth. On reporting for work on *Meet Me in St. Louis*, she handed these over to her new make-up artist, Dotty Ponedel. 'What are these?' asked Ponedel. Garland explained and Ponedel responded, 'You don't need all this junk. You're a pretty girl.' She then made minimal adjustments and, for the first time on-screen, Garland – who from then on insisted that Ponedel worked with her – looked lovely.

Minnelli made her look even lovelier. Although *Meet Me in St. Louis* has a sustained and flowing rhythm throughout; although Minnelli paid all necessary attention to every detail and to every performer; although he not only gave Margaret O'Brien a long, sustained sequence of her own but fought successfully to retain it when it was under threat of removal; all the same, he turned *Meet Me in St. Louis* into a love letter to Judy Garland.

Just as the opening shot of each of the seasonal segments was framed like a greetings card, so, over and over again, Garland herself was framed as in a greetings card. In the Trolley Song she was framed by a circle composed of the decorated hats of the other young women on the trolley-car. At other times she was framed in windows, in mirrors, in a door-frame, by a trellis, by artfully cast shadows. She was shown to superb advantage in luminous close-ups, and she was given freer reign to act, both humorously and dramatically, than ever before. She was the focal point of a lovely succession of patterns which were constantly shifting and re-forming. Never was she to owe a director more than she owed Minnelli, and never, apart from her performances in *The Clock* and *The Pirate* (both again for Minnelli) and in *A Star is Born* (with George Cukor at last in charge of a film for her) did she, by her performance, repay her debt more amply.

All these favours, all this attention, and even her own eventual total commitment to the project did not mean that her conduct was

Judy: framed by hats –

perfect; far from it. Her tantrums, her temperament, her tardiness, her hypochondria, her possibly genuine ailments, tested everyone's patience, and led to remonstrations from Minnelli and Freed as well as the ticking-off from Mary Astor. She delayed the shooting of the movie for thirteen days, all told, and was responsible (with O'Brien) for putting the film far behind schedule, and costing her studio a great deal of wasted money. However, she made the studio a great deal more money both with this film and subsequently – until, six years later, its patience finally ran out. Garland's film career only really began with MGM and, even though she made four more films after leaving the studio, it as good as ended when she was sacked by MGM in the early stages of filming *Annie Get Your Gun* (of which melancholy traces were to be seen in the 1994 compilation movie *That's Entertainment! III*).

At 47 she was dead, a victim of drink, drugs, failed marriages and exploitation by those who sought to make money out of her extraordinary talent. Everyone who saw her work paid testimony to that talent. Long after their marriage, long after Garland had thwarted further projects on which he could have collaborated with her to the advantage of both of them, Vincente Minnelli recalled: 'The surface wasn't scratched with Judy at all. She had great potential. She could

– Framed in doorways

have done anything she wanted, as great as Duse or Bernhardt or Garbo. You could tell her twenty things and you'd never know if you were getting through to her or not, because people were messing with her and making her up and so forth. And by God, everything was in place. She wouldn't forget a thing.'

It was not only Judy Garland's career that was stunted. So was her life. One of the contract dancers in *Meet Me in St. Louis* remembered, 'She was without doubt the greatest talent I've ever worked with. She would pick up a script and read it for the first time, and she'd read it like she's studied it for two weeks.' The memory of another dancer was more poignant still: 'I remember her telling us one time that if she had it to do again she would like her life to take her the way it had, except she would have liked a childhood. The one thing that she regretted for Margaret O'Brien when we were on *Meet Me in St. Louis* – because Margaret was a little girl – and she said, "This poor child isn't having a childhood", and she said, "That's the one thing I would change in my life."'

Full of regrets and yet capable of portraying and bestowing joy, in *Meet Me in St. Louis* Garland left behind her this unalloyed treasure, all sunshine and happiness with not the tiniest overt sign of the storms and sadness to come.

## FEELING GOOD

When, at the Odeon, Leicester Square, London in 1977, the final images at the premiere of *Close Encounters of the Third Kind* faded from the screen, the audience refused to move. They simply sat there, wishing the film could go on. It was not just that the Spielberg movie had so enchanted them that they wanted to bask in its afterglow. They knew that what they had seen was merely a captivating fiction and that, out there, there were no benign extraterrestrials and exalted humans but simply the same old harsh world, with its mixture of happy moments and problems and miseries.

Although movies, even the sad and challenging ones, are escapism, the happiest movies are in a way the most precarious species of escapism. The poignancy of 'feel-good' pictures is that, even while we are watching them and cherishing them, we know that they are not true.

*Meet Me in St. Louis* is more untrue than feel-good films of scientific imaginativeness like *Close Encounters of the Third Kind* and *E.T.*, and more untrue than feel-good films of the supernatural like *Field of Dreams*. We accept (most of us, at any rate) that there are no extraterrestrials and we know that there are no unseen forces that can reward a man's longings with the baseball pitch of his imaginings.

On the other hand, we know that there was a St. Louis in the first decade of the twentieth century and that it was home to the Exposition, preparations for which are the substructure of the plot of *Meet Me in St. Louis*. We know, too, that there was a family, the Benson family of Sally, author of the Kensington Avenue stories, which was the real-life counterpart of the fictional Smith family. Yet, without having known the Benson family as well as we come to know the Smiths during their 110 minutes of screen time, we do know that their life cannot have been as placid and cosy as that of the Smiths. They will have had quarrels; they will have had difficulties far more serious than the contretemps over whether the family was going to be uprooted and move to New York (a problem solved in the film, without a single disquieting or unsettling repercussion, in the flame of an idly struck match). The Benson–Smiths will have had permanent partings and illnesses and bereavements. They will have been a real family, rather than the fictional dwellers in paradise whom we as spectators take to our hearts on the screen and whom we so wish not to let go that we treasure them half a century after the Freed–Minnelli movie told us about them.

There were quarrels in the original stories on which the film was based. Freed and his scriptwriters erased them. In the book the family's mother lost her temper. The earth-mother of the Finklehoffe–Brecher screenplay never loses her temper and, when she and the rest of the family get upset at her husband's decision to move to New York, it is she who is the prime mover in reuniting the family, by taking her seat at the piano as her husband and she sing 'You and I'; she calms the discontent and forces the family to accept their father's decision with good grace.

The original lyric for another song, 'Have Yourself a Merry Little Christmas', which actually envisaged a permanent parting, was rewritten with more comforting words. Although Harry Davenport, who played Grandfather Prophater, was 77 at the time the movie was made, the only intimations of death relate not to him but to children's games. Tootie is cute, not ominous, when she tells the iceman at the beginning of the film that her doll is mortally ill and has 'got to go'. When she hears that the family have to move to New York her immediate reaction is to announce, 'I'm taking all my dolls – the dead ones, too'; and she goes on to explain, 'It'll take me at least a week to dig up all my dolls from the cemetery.' Agnes hopes Father Christmas will bring her a hunting knife for Christmas, but we know that she would not know what to do with a hunting knife if she got one.

To audiences half a century after the film was made the most remarkable episode is one that causes a brief upset, but no more than that. After her Hallowe'en adventure, Tootie returns home injured and wailing, alleging that John Truett has attacked her. Such a turn of events in a 1990s movie would have led to a sensational reaction. Child abuse! A grown man attacking a six-year-old girl! The doctor would have been summoned immediately, not simply to tend the injury and provide comforting words, but to examine the child for sexual interference. When Tootie is examined, a tuft of John Truett's hair is found in her fist. The doctor comments, 'It must have been quite a struggle fighting him off'; yet, despite this apparent evidence of a serious assault on a small girl by a mature male, no official action is taken. In a comparable situation in a 1990s movie, not only the doctor would have been summoned; the police would have been called, too. Truett would have been arrested and, instead of a punch from Esther that turned into a reconciliation, any possibility of a happy relationship between him and Esther would have been ended permanently.

In the film as we know it, however, the reaction is relaxed to the point of placidity. The police – who do not exist as far as this film is concerned, not surprisingly since the St. Louis of 1903–4 appears to be crime-free – remain unsummoned. The mother is a little put out by Tootie's story, but nothing more. The only person who gets at all angry is Esther, who engages in that bout of fisticuffs with Truett which is entirely to his satisfaction. The film is preternaturally innocent.

The world of *Meet Me in St. Louis* is not one in which men attack small children, or in which such a possibility can even be contemplated. It is a world in which no one is profoundly unhappy, or is unhappy in any way for very long. No one is poor, no one is homeless, no one is nasty. The original material contained characters involved in marital infidelity; they were removed from the narrative. Mr Braukoff may be regarded by the children as a monster whom Tootie must be courageous enough to kill on Hallowe'en; and, photographed from the upward-looking angle providing the little girl's subjective point of view, he does indeed look frightening. Once she has run off to proclaim her triumph, however, a less distorted camera viewpoint shows us that he is simply an ordinary, good-natured fellow, while his apparently terrifying bulldog placidly laps up the flour that Tootie has thrown.

This is a film about a cosy, comforting refuge: the Smith home. A few scenes take place elsewhere: on the trolley-car, in the street during Hallowe'en, on the porch of the Truett neighbours (a family which, apart from John, does not seem to exist), and at the Exposition site as the movie ends. All the rest of the film is set inside the Smiths' house, in their yard, and in the street immediately outside. Scenes set in Alonzo Smith's office, at his cribbage game, and on a visit outside St. Louis to the Smith grandparents, were excised.

The concentration on this warm, cosy and nestlike home is no accident. Inside the nest are the mother and her chicks, with the mock-grumpy father out earning the salary that keeps them in such comfort. The family does everything together – eats together, goes to the ball together, goes to the Exposition together. The film is in fact about the warmth of an enfolding and enveloping home, and its theme is very deliberate. Arthur Freed explained, 'What I wanted to make was a simple story, a story that basically says, "There's no place like home."' It is no accident that home is where E.T., in a film made by the ultimate nostalgia-movie buff Spielberg, longed to get to. It is no coincidence that these very words are the final and explanatory sentence spoken by Dorothy to Aunt Em in Freed's other classic film starring Judy Garland, *The Wizard of Oz*.

*The Wizard of Oz* is literally about nostalgia, a word which means the pain associated with wishing to return to the past. Throughout the film Dorothy, despite having landed in a captivating country crammed with marvellous apparitions, has only one objective – to get back home: a surprising objective since, back home, Miss Gulch is waiting to murder Dorothy's dog Toto.

In *Meet Me in St. Louis*, four Dorothys – Rose, Esther, Agnes, Tootie – are already at home, together with parents, brother, grandfather, cat and amiable, jokey servant who is really one of the family. Their objective is not to get back home, but to stay there. The wonderful surprise for them all at the end of the film is that they are indeed going to stay and that their perfect world is not going to change in any way. A happy ending is promised for Esther's romance with John Truett, but that ending is not shown in the film since it would mean the break-up of the family. If Esther married her dream-boy-next-door there would be no one to plot with Rose and to be a second mother to Tootie.

This film is immaculate because it does not envisage a life – or death – for any of the characters after the end-title. If such a technique had then been available, maybe Minnelli would have ended it with a freeze-frame, as Truffaut was, for very different purposes, to do with *Les Quatre Cents Coups* fifteen years later. Meanwhile the family carries on with its small, satisfying rituals, tasting the ketchup, eating the cake, sharing meals around the laden table.

In 1944 a film like this fed hunger. Families were broken up because of the war. Fathers were often away, often abroad, defending their country, risking their lives, maybe losing their lives – maybe having affairs with women not their wives. Mothers were often out of the home, too, working in factories to supply war weapons for their absent husbands. At an army camp, at an urban cinema after a day's hard work, a film so warm and comforting offered balm and offered hope: hope that the postwar world could be something like this even if the prewar world had never been quite like this – or like this at all.

My family in Leeds, even bigger than the Smiths' – there were seven of us children – had been broken up by the war. Several of us had been evacuated. My brother, the husbands of two of my sisters and the boyfriend of a third were all abroad at the fighting front. I remember first seeing *Meet Me in St. Louis* at a local cinema, the Clock, and feeling happy and soothed after it was over, as I came out into the blacked-out streets and went home to listen to the war news on the radio.

Today the film provides a double nostalgia. Turn-of-the-century St. Louis seems almost intolerably attractive in a world of nuclear weapons, of Aids, of urban crime (in which parents would think carefully before allowing their children out into the streets alone to celebrate Hallowe'en, instead of, as in the movie, dressing them up, equipping them with flour, and speeding them on their way); of high divorce rates; of single mothers who may never have married; of convenience frozen foods rather than home-made dishes flavoured by home-made ketchup; of unemployment rather than breadwinners so secure in their jobs that without a qualm they can afford to turn down a promotion; of child abuse; of poor public transport rather than a reliable and clean trolley service. We feel almost intolerable nostalgia for those lost days.

We feel nostalgia, too, for the time when *Meet Me in St. Louis* was filmed at MGM: by a studio system that no longer exists to make such movies, at a studio which no longer contains a vast backlot on which to build such a huge, elaborate set, with no almost limitless list of contract players to provide such a perfect cast. The time when *Meet Me in St. Louis* was filmed is further away from us today than, to those who filmed it, was the time in which it was set. Even though a war was being waged at the time it was conceived and completed, even though terrible events were then taking place which we did not know about at the time but which we know about now, 1944 seems to us a safer time than today. We yearn not only for the warmth of 1904 but for the confidence and clarity of life in 1944. It is impossible to imagine developments in the future that will be so heartening as to make us not wish or need any longer to spend an hour and fifty minutes with the Smith family in Kensington Avenue.

How happy they were throughout the film, and how especially happy they were as the film came to an end! The last words in Sally Benson's book are faithfully reflected at the close of the picture.

ROSE: There never has been anything like it in this world. There never will be.

MRS SMITH: And just think. It's all right here where we live.

AGNES: It's where we live. We don't have to visit here. We don't have to come on a train, or stay at a hotel, or anything. They won't ever tear it down, will they?

TOOTIE: No. They will never tear it down. It will be like this forever.

AGNES: I can't believe it. Right here where we live. Right here in St. Louis.

Freed, reading those words, could not possibly have resisted making the film. 'They will never tear it down': permanency. 'Right here where we live': in the place that no other place is like – home. And in a state of bliss frozen in permanency: forever. Happiness forever. That is what a feel-good movie is all about. That is the secret at the heart of the reassurance that *Meet Me in St. Louis* provides to all of us, a reassurance for which we yearn while, at the same time, knowing that it can never be.

# CREDITS

. . . . . . . . . . . . . . . . . . . . . . . . .

## Meet Me in St. Louis

**USA**
1944
**Production company**
Loew's Incorporated
**US release**
31 December 1944
**US Distributor**
Metro-Goldwyn-Mayer
Pictures
**GB release**
19 March 1945
**GB distributor**
Metro-Goldwyn-Mayer
Pictures
**Producer**
Arthur Freed
**Director**
Vincente Minnelli
**Assistant director**
Wallace Worsley
**Screenplay**
Irving Brecher, Fred F.
Finklehoffe from the novel
by Sally Benson
**Uncredited script
contributions**
Sally Benson, Doris Gilbert,
Sarah Y. Mason, Victor
Heerman, William Ludwig
**Photography
(Technicolor)**
George Folsey (uncredited:
Harold Rosson for 'The
Trolley Song' sequence)
**Technicolor colour
director**
Natalie Kalmus
**Associate Technicolor
colour director**
Henri Jaffa

**Musical director**
George Stoll
**Uncredited musical
director**
Lennie Hayton
**Musical adaptation**
Roger Edens
**Orchestration**
Conrad Salinger
**Songs**
'The Trolley Song', 'The
Boy Next Door', 'Skip to
my Lou', 'Have Yourself a
Merry Little Christmas' by
Hugh Martin, Ralph Blane;
'Under the Bamboo Tree' by
Bob Cole, J. Rosamond
Johnson; 'Meet Me in St.
Louis' by Andrew B.
Sterling, Kerry Mills; 'You
and I' by Arthur Freed,
Nacio Herb Brown; 'I Was
Drunk Last Night', 'Over
the Bannister' (traditional)
arranged by Conrad
Salinger; 'Brighten the
Corner' by Charles H.
Gabriel Jr.; 'Summer in St.
Louis', 'The Invitation' by
Roger Edens; 'All Hallow's
Eve', 'The Horrible One',
'Ah, Love!' by Conrad
Salinger; 'Good-bye My
Lady Love' by Joe Howard;
'Under the Anheuser Bush'
by Albert von Tilzer; 'Little
Brown Jug' by R. A.
Eastburn, arranged by
Lennie Hayton; 'The Fair'
by Lennie Hayton
**Dance director**
Charles Walters

**Editor**
Albert Akst
**Art directors**
Cedric Gibbons, Lemuel
Ayers, Jack Martin Smith
**Set decorator**
Edwin B. Willis
**Associate set decorator**
Paul Huldchinsky
**Costume designer**
Sharaff
**Costume supervisor**
Irene
**Make-up**
Jack Dawn
**Recording director**
Douglas Shearer
**Sound recording**
Joe Edmondson
**113 minutes**
10,147 ft

**Judy Garland**
*Esther Smith*
**Margaret O'Brien**
*'Tootie' Smith*
**Mary Astor**
*Mrs Anna Smith*
**Lucille Bremer**
*Rose Smith*
**Leon Ames**
*Alonzo Smith*
**Tom Drake**
*John Truett*
**Marjorie Main**
*Katie the maid*
**Harry Davenport**
*Grandpa*
**June Lockhart**
*Lucille Ballard*
**Henry H. Daniels Jr**
*Lon Smith Jr*
**Joan Carroll**
*Agnes Smith*
**Hugh Marlowe**
*Colonel Darly*
**Robert Sully**
*Warren Sheffield*
**Chill Wills**
*Mr Neely*
**Donald Curtis**
*Dr Terry*
**Mary Jo Ellis**
*Ida Boothby*
**Ken Wilson**
*Quentin*
**Robert Emmett O'Connor**
*Motorman*
**Darryl Hickman**
*Johnny Tevis*
**Leonard Walker**
*Conductor*
**Victor Kilian**
*Baggage man*
**John Phipps**
*Mailman*
**Major Sam Harris**
*Mr March*

**Mayo Newhall**
*Mr Braukoff*
**Belle Mitchell**
*Mrs Braukoff*
**Sidney Barnes**
*Hugo Borvis*
**Myron Tobias**
*George*
**Victor Cox**
*Driver*
**Joe Cobbs**
**Kenneth Donner**
**Buddy Gorman**
*Clinton Badgers*
**Helen Gilbert**
*Girl on trolley*
**Arthur Freed**
*Singing voice of Alonzo Smith*
**D. Markas**
*Singing voice of Anna Smith*

Credits compiled by Markku Salmi. Print acquired from Turner Entertainment specially for the Classics series. Available on the MGM Musicals label from Warner Home Video.

# BIBLIOGRAPHY

. . . . . . . . . . . . . . . . . . . . . . .

Sally Benson, *Meet Me in St. Louis* (New York: Random House, 1942).

Joseph Andrew Casper, *Vincente Minnelli and the Film Musical* (London: Yoseloff, 1977).

Hugh Fordin, *The World of Entertainment*! (New York: Doubleday, 1975).

Stephen Harvey, *Directed by Vincente Minnelli* (New York: Museum of Modern Art, 1989).

John Houseman, *Front and Center* (New York: Touchstone, 1980).

Vincente Minnelli with Hector Arce, *I Remember It Well* (London: Angus and Robertson, 1975).

Richard Schickel, *The Men Who Made the Movies* (London: Elm Tree Books, 1977).

David Shipman, *Judy Garland* (London: Fourth Estate, 1992).

# ALSO PUBLISHED

**If you would like further information about future BFI Film Classics or about other books on film, media and popular culture from BFI Publishing, please write to:**

**BFI Film Classics**
**British Film Institute**
**21 Stephen Street**
**London**
**W1P 1PL**